WE ARE ALL KINGS

NYEEAM HUDSON

ISBN: 13-978-1542418799

DEDICATION

This book is dedicated to my mother and father,
my sister and brothers; my family
I LOVE YOU!

To my supporters, your contributions made this
book possible.
Your belief in me will help me motivate and
inspire
all the children around the world.
THANK YOU!

ACKNOWLEDGMENTS

Sylvester Wofford – Illustrator
P. Renae Brooks – Editor
Al-Tariq Best – Mentor
Andrew Grandison – Mentor

To all media who allowed me the opportunity to share my motivational messages around the world.

Parent's Guide to Help Motivate Your Child's Greatness

My purpose in creating *We Are All Kings* is to motivate and inspire all young men across the world, and let them know that anything is possible if you just believe in yourself.

I am asking parents and teachers to please read about my actual journey to your children or students.

The story of my journey will impact the children the most. I want them to see that I am a growing child just like they are, achieving my dreams at a young age.

Thank you for supporting my motivational messages and inspiring your child to achieve their greatness!

NYEEAM'S JOURNEY

*"Expose your child to a broad spectrum of experiences.
Let them explore and tap into their greatness –
every moment counts!"* – Nyeeam Hudson

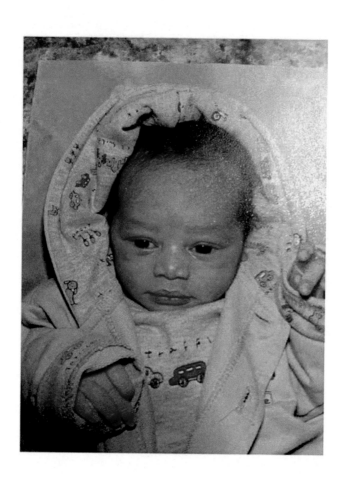

My Beginning

My baby picture, yeah that's right. I was having a difficult time trying to figure out how I wanted to start my book, and then everything clicked. I decided I'll start the beginning of the book with the beginning of my life.

In this picture I was only a few days old. Of course I don't really remember much, but my father told me I was a quiet baby. I would just sit back and observe everything. And that's so funny, because as an eleven-year-old I find myself doing the same thing. Looking around trying to figure out the world in my head, but I'm sure that's something that all children can relate to. That's why the beginning of a child's life is so important.

We download everything we see. We may not understand everything in the moment, but your whispers and smiles in all of your daily activities will become the foundation of our imagination.

Imagination

Imagination is so important to children because children can't get up and go where they want. So for us to do the things we want to do, sometimes we have to imagine it and picture it in our mind.

When we start creating pictures in our mind, we take the pictures from our everyday surroundings, like the television, our house, our neighborhood.

So it's very important for you to show your children as many great things as possible. Read a lot of different books to them, listen to different music, travel and let them see different environments. All of this will help your children be creative and have a beautiful imagination.

Traveling the World

Traveling the world is a beautiful thing. You learn a lot and you get exposed to so many things you didn't know. I just want to let all the children know to never be afraid to travel.

I want you to get a notebook and write down three places you want to visit. Make sure you research the new places and don't stop until you make that dream happen!

My first trip was to North Carolina. I was so excited to be on an airplane! It's amazing when you take off and see how small the buildings get. You don't really feel anything in the air. Most of the time I just sit back and listen to my music.

Africa was my longest flight, it took 17 hours, but the cool thing about that trip were the televisions and video games on the plane, so everything seemed pretty fast for me.

Building Confidence

What would I do without the mirror? Singing and dancing in the mirror every day was a big self-esteem booster for me.

The mirror was my audience, the mirror was my television. If I could do a good job in the mirror, then I know I can do a good job on stage. Even though I used to make a lot of noise every day, my father never told me to sit down or be quiet.

He let me find my voice, and sometimes he got up and danced in the mirror with me. And I know that may seem like a small gesture, but that did so much for my confidence. It taught me to never be afraid. It taught me to be free.

So even when I'm on stage in front of thousands of people, it still feels like I'm just dancing in the mirror.

Helping Others

You never know who needs a little push, a spark of inspiration. You could be one day away from the motivation that will change your life forever.

It feels so good writing my first book. I know this book will help millions of young men all around the world. Putting this book together helped me in so many ways. I still can't believe I can turn pages and read my own story!

I want you to know you have the same power. Whatever your story is I guarantee you, your journey can help so many other young men, and all it takes is that spark, that spark of belief, that spark of confidence.

Don't wait for the world to tell you how great you are. Look in the mirror and tell yourself you got this. I am a king and my mind is my crown! I will pick my friends up and not tear them down.

Bullying

Bullying is a global issue and it affects so many children around the world. But every time this problem is brought up, I think we focus on the problems a little too much. We need to create solutions and get to the root of what causes children to bully.

I look at bullying like a volcano. Volcanoes don't erupt overnight, volcanoes go through a process before they explode. So just like volcanoes I think we should figure out the process to what makes bullies explode.

A lack of love, a lack of attention, a young_man crying-out for help but nobody's there, mental or physical abuse. These are some of the things that build up and makes bullies explode.

With more love and more communication we will create so many solutions for bullying. Every bully has a voice. We should take the time to hear their story, and in their story we will find solutions.

Don't Kill the Noise

If I asked you how does a baby talk, most people would say *'goo goo gaga'* and I wouldn't say they're wrong, but it's so many ways babies communicate. Babies communicate with their eyes, babies communicate with their facial expressions. It's beautiful and amazing watching a new life figure it all out. Most people would say babies cry too much and children make too much noise. Well here is the lesson! Noise is everything! Noise is the language to a child that doesn't know how to speak yet.

I remember watching videos of myself when I was four years old, and it looked like I was just running around making noise. I asked my father why he didn't just tell me to sit down and be quiet. He told me making that noise was the pinnacle of my happiness. He paused the video and told me to look at my eyes, that's where the confidence is.

If you kill the noise you kill the confidence. The words will come but never tamper with the foundation of the confidence.

Parenting

It's very important for parents to believe in their children. When you tell your children how great they are and consistently show them appreciation every day, it's going to be hard for anyone to try to knock them down.

Parents are every child's first superhero. So if your hero believes in you then you will start to build an unstoppable confidence.

And it works the opposite way as well. If parents don't believe in their children then it's going to be hard to make your children believe in themselves. It starts with you guys. Create a powerful environment that allows your children to grow.

I am Learning New Things

Don't be afraid to learn something new. That's one of the most important things you have to understand once you start traveling. There are so many different cultures and communities around the world, even the everyday things that we find to be normal.

I remember when I was in Mexico and I was flipping a quarter and I told them to do heads or tails. They looked at me confused because they did not know what I was taking about. Over there when you flip a coin its eagle or sun, and that's what I mean when I say learning new things.

That's a small example but it shows you how the everyday things we find so normal are totally different once you travel.

Building Your Brand

Once children believe in themselves enough, they're going to do everything with love and happiness. So everything that's inside them will come out with their creativity.

Support them and invest in their ideas. Help them build a positive brand around their happiness.

That love and confidence will help inspire other children around the world. *We Are All Kings* is my personal example.

I am living the advice I'm sharing with you.

Positive Friends

We all have different perspectives on the things we love and the things we like. So many people don't achieve their dreams because their friends didn't agree with their ideas.

When I first started motivational speaking, none of my friends even knew what motivational speaking was. Some children said it was corny, it wasn't popular, but I didn't let that stop me. I had a vision and I just kept going.

I want you to do the same thing! If you want to be a doctor, if you want to be a basketball player, if you want to be a scientist, don't let your friends get in the way of your dreams.

Keep going until you make your vision real. Pick positive friends that push you toward to your dreams.

Just Be a Kid

Now these words are definitely dream killers! *"Just be a kid."* I understand what adults mean, but let's dive into these words a little further.

It's no one way to be a kid. Some kids play with toys. Some kids read books all day. Some kids play sports. There are no kid rules.

Traveling around the world I see so many different concepts of what we call kids, and me being a kid myself, I think children should be free to find their own happiness. Some days I want to go to the park, some days I want to read, and some days I want to stand on stage and inspire the world.

All of these things bring me happiness. But for some reason I keep hearing people say that I should just focus on being a kid. It confuses me because I don't know what that means.

Don't block your child's happiness. Let them define what a kid means to them. It's no one way to be a kid.

Always Express Yourself

Every time I see one of my friends his head is always down. I ask him *'What's wrong?'* He always says *'I'm sad'* and I say *'No! Tell me what's going on with you!'* and then he said *'I'm mad!'*

It took me some time to think about it, but I figured it out. My friend doesn't know how to express himself. He doesn't have the words in his vocabulary to tell me, or himself, exactly how he feels. Every feeling has a word that describes that feeling, but he didn't have enough words in his mind to express how he felt in his heart.

This is what causes a lot of young men to walk around angry. By telling this story I'm hoping these words will help you understand what young men go through, so we can figure out ways to help build them up.

But if you're a young man going through something like this, don't be afraid to express yourself the best way you know how. It's okay to cry. It's okay to hug and start dealing with the pain one day at a time.

Negativity

Don't take other people's opinions personal. Sometimes people will joke with you not knowing how bad it actually hurts you inside.

Sometime we do the same thing not knowing that we hurt other people.

Negativity is anything that's not lifting another person up. So think about the words that come out of your mouth before you say them to one of your friends.

Conquer Your Journey to Read

This is a reading trick that my father did with me. When I was in third grade I didn't like reading. I didn't understand it. But this is how my father got me to fall in love with reading. He knew that I liked superheroes and Ninja Turtles. So he took me to the library and let me pick all the fun books with my favorite characters in them. I was so excited to pick up books with things I can identify with because that's what I was interested in. I would read them every day. But the trick was that I starting to enjoy reading.

I tell some of my friends to think about reading books and updating your mind like updating a video game. The more you know the more things you can do. I learn something new every day. Why? Because I challenge myself to read, read and read! If you are struggling with reading, math or just learning, dedicate yourself and don't give up. It may be a little frustrating sometimes, but it's not official if you don't cry and push forward. Keep your focus on the goal – don't give up! You can never be defeated as long as you are learning!

Support System

When you're trying to accomplish your dream, make sure you surround yourself with people that believes in you. People that help push you forward even when you get discouraged and you need them to inspire you.

Stay away from the people that say you can't make it. People like that are going to do nothing but bring you down. Sometimes you might have to be the voice that reminds yourself to keep pushing.

In the beginning my father didn't want me to do what I'm doing now. It wasn't that he didn't want to support me, he just didn't see my vision all the way. In the beginning of my journey, I didn't know exactly what I wanted to do, but I knew he loved me enough that if I kept going he would eventually support me.

So your support may come from different people, maybe your mother, father, friends or school teacher. Wherever the people are that believes in you make sure you keep them around.

Environment

Never let your environment make you feel like you can't accomplish something. The most amazing thing about the internet is that you can research and see how many different stories about how some successful people came from some pretty difficult situations. But most of the time all we see is the success.

There is something I want you to do. If you look-up to someone, I want you to research their story so you can understand that you're not the only one going through hard times. Keep your head up, make sure you don't let your crown fall.

If no one believes in you, I want to let you know that I believe in you! *We Are All Kings!* Keep repeating that to yourself until you make your dreams come true.

Advice to all Fathers

When a man truly loves his children, he will never make excuses. My father grew up in a foster home and never knew his father. He didn't know how to read until he was 17-years old.

It really makes me sad when I hear my father's story. But, he told me that all the pain he went through made him the man he is today!

So, if I can give any advice to all of the fathers out there, I would say 'Never let your pain make you run away. Allow your pain to make you stronger and let painful experiences help you to be there for your children.'

Encanta su

Motiva a estudiantes
charla de 'King Nahh',
de sólo 9 años,
en el congreso
Empredil

IMELDA ROBLES

Entre cientos de asistentes, "King Nahh" es el de más baja estatura.

DE VIAJE

ST. BARTHS,
DE LUJO
El azul intenso
de sus aguas
y su íntimo
ambiente han
convertido a
esta isla en la
consentida de
celebridades.
Pág. 14

VIDA
ES UN GRAN
MOTIVADOR
DE SÓLO
¡9 AÑOS!
Pág. 11

HEROÍNAS
EN LOS CÓMICS

einorte.com

Motivation

If I had a quarter for every time I heard, *"You're a kid! What do you know?"* – I would be rich! Lol... But on a serious note, one thing I do know is that there is no age requirement for spreading motivation; it can come from anyone at any time.

I had to motivate myself when no one believed in a little kid with a dream. I had to take action and show improvement. My little dream was just in my head, and if I wanted to make it real I had to work for it.

Never Give Up

You never know what your journey means to other people. I'm sure it's someone out there, somewhere, that believes in what you're doing. So whatever your talent is or whatever your dreams are, I want you to continue and never stop.

Whenever you hear that voice in your head telling you how great you are, that's your subconscious mind telling you something that it already knows. Your greatness belongs to the people you're supposed to inspire. I want you to say *'I am great and I can conquer anything I put my mind to!'*

A puzzle can have a thousand pieces but it's not complete until you put the last puzzle piece in the puzzle. You never know what your dream is connected to! Just keep going!

Inspire People

Have the courage to tell your story. Your life may be simple to you, your pain may hurt you inside, your downfall may be sad to you, but you never know who your story will inspire and in the process of inspiring others you will find happiness.

Every day I get hundreds of messages telling me how my video clips changed other people's lives. And it's still overwhelming to me that a simple little video that you record on your phone can touch millions of people all around the world. So I just want to encourage you to inspire others and let your journey help someone else.

Thank You!

THANK YOU so much for believing in me and for actually taking the time to read my book! If you have ever watched one of my YouTube videos, if you have ever shared my posts, or wrote a comment on any one of my social media networks, I just want to THANK YOU from the bottom of my heart.

This is my first book and I promise you I will get better as I keep producing. I hope the messages in this book motivates and inspires all the children and parents around the world.

Stay tuned I'm working on two more books *We Are All Queens* and *My Motivational Journey*.

Again, THANK YOU! I truly appreciate your support!

Write Your Story

My name is King_____

_____

_____

_____

_____

_____

_____

_____

_____

_____

_____

_____

_____

ABOUT THE AUTHOR

As a youth-advocate and spokesperson, Nyeeam Hudson *'King Nahh'* has engaged in numerous conversations and has been an invited guest keynote speaker across the states and the globe speaking loudly and proudly against violence, delivering motivational messages of peace, love, and happiness. Nyeeam has travelled to Dubai, Saudi Arabia; Tanzania, Africa and Monterrey, Mexico.

We Are All Kings is a heartfelt message to every

young male in the world to encourage them to believe in themselves as kings of greatness. Nyeeam is working on national school tours. His goal is to motivate, inspire and deliver words of encouragement, while personally reading his works, making new friends across the globe,

and most importantly he wants to crown each of them *We Are All Kings*. Nyeeam unselfishly understands the power of positive thinking and simply wants to give back.

Made in the USA
San Bernardino, CA
23 August 2018